# Inside Out

a better way of living, learning, and loving

## DADI JANKI

BRAHMA KUMARIS

Inside *Out*
A Better Way of Living, Learning and Loving

Author Dadi Janki

Compiled and edited by Neville Hodgkinson

3rd Edition, 2009
4th Edition, 2013
5th Edition, 2016

ISBN No. 978-1-886872-26-4

Published by Brahma Kumaris Information Services Ltd.,
Global Co-operation House, 65 Pound Lane, London NW10 2HH, UK

Website: www.inspiredstillness.com
E-mail: hello@inspiredstillness.com

Designed by infograf.co.uk
Printed in India by Imprint Press

Preface

# Preface

**'What type of world would I like to see tomorrow morning?'**

By Alfredo Sfeir Younis\*

We are living in a world of major awakening. It is very important to understand that we are not only part of the experience of this awakening, but that we happen to be the architects.

I often ask myself the question: 'How would I like to wake up tomorrow morning? What would be my ideal awakening? What would I like my eyes to see?'

Sooner or later we will all agree on what this awakening is about. We want a world free from poverty, from crime, from racism, a world full of equality and understanding, where people are happy, a world without environmental destruction, a world of social stability. A world with a new identity. A world of a new beginning.

---

\* Senior Adviser, The World Bank. The views expressed here are solely those of the author and should not be attributed to the World Bank or any of its affiliates. Errors and omissions are solely of the author's.

If that is the world we want to wake up to tomorrow morning, what do we have to do today? Why is it that we cannot find that world?

We don't have to create this new world. We have to become this new world. We have to change again and again to be able to awaken one day into that world which we are all waiting for. The tragedy of humanity is that this beautiful world is already there and yet somehow we don't grab it, we don't see it.

Despite the Shakespearian tragedy many people seem to live every day, someone and something, somewhere, keeps this world going. It is as though a high-speed train is coming towards us - we feel bad about it, we are unhappy, we are depressed - but somehow our arms are still here, and the flowers are still blooming. Someone and something is beyond all of this.

I believe this someone and something, that is keeping things going, is both material and non-material (spiritual). This is why I am always searching for people who embody these material and non-material elements. The souls who are essentially the golden thread that keeps the quilt of humanity clean and warm, every night, every time, in spite of everything else.

One of the most enlightened people walking with us in this world today is Dadi Janki. I think it is amazing that I have had the privilege to live at the same time as her. It is a pleasure and a privilege to offer this preface to her latest book.

At the material level she exists as a woman, and at the non-material (spiritual) level she sits at the point of pure awareness. On the one hand, the pure awareness serves as the golden thread for all humanity and on the other hand, she does the same things that we do every day like eating, chatting, teaching, sleeping. This incredibly profound and subtle, double dimension is like the two sides of a precious coin that we have here at hand.

Dadi Janki is so important to the world. This importance goes beyond her material existence. She is such a soul that no matter what state she is in physically, she will continue to thread the human quilt so as to awaken us to a better future for humanity.

My relationship with Dadi Janki has been very enriching and there are a number of elements in her way of being that I would like to share with you.

# 1. Dadi Janki is a trustee of the purity of knowledge.

The purity of knowledge is at the essence of this golden thread that Dadi Janki is. The beauty of such knowledge is that it is very simple. Her words find the most intimate space in our hearts and souls.

This is an essential lesson that we should learn: that it is not a matter of being only spiritual, but we need to be trustees of the purity of knowledge. It is not just a matter of knowing, it is a matter of what we really self-realise, and how that knowledge makes us live our life in a particular way.

One of the most interesting things in my conversations with Dadi Janki is the high degree of consistency. It is not like one mixed salad of things today, and another mixed salad tomorrow. She is clear and I understand her paradigm exactly. Each meeting gives me an opportunity to see a piece of the puzzle, knowing what the paradigm is all about. It is not like being on automatic pilot, but rather you are sitting with your hands firmly on the steering wheel, knowing there is a road map.

## 2. Dadi Janki embodies spiritual transformational value.

A spiritual teacher or leader is only so if he or she has a transformational value. You would be able to recognise that person as a teacher because they have transformed your life by their mere existence. Others can speak well, they can give knowledge, but that is not everything.

After I first met Dadi Janki, I experienced her transformational value. And such value must be the icon for all of us. She has not the exclusivity of it. This universal transforming value should also become the engine and ultimate ingredient that moves all institutions in our society, because, in the end, institutions are people. These institutions would not exist if it were not for professionals and people like you and me. Factories don't exist without the human content. Governments don't exist without people.

If you were to ask a political party: 'Do you want to create poverty?' they would say: 'Of course not.' 'Do you want to degrade the environment?' 'No, of course not.' If you were to go to a church and ask the same questions, the answers would be the same. Nobody says they want to create poverty, crime, drug abuse, depression, unhappiness, frustration, etc. But the fact is that we have lost the ability to maintain unified and holistic values when we move from the abstract (the ideal) to the concrete (the reality). There is a breakdown in the ability of our society to maintain unity in the values of existence from the abstract to the concrete. The abstract is what I want to wake up to tomorrow morning. And the concrete is the actual reality of what we see everyday vis-à-vis those values.

If I asked someone: 'Do you love?', she/he would answer: 'Yes, I love.' But actually love is a state of being we need to share as a matter of self-realisation, particularly in times of conflict. Love needs to be where there is not. Spirituality needs to be where there is none. However, few have self-realised these states of being, and thus we do not have the ability to share spiritual love with those we dislike, oppose and hate. In the same vein, we talk about equality, inclusion, fraternity, sharing and caring, but we have not experienced these values to share them in the most critical moments.

Dadi Janki has no breakdown between her abstract and her concrete, no matter where she moves. Very few human beings possess such a high ability to maintain this holistic unity in this way, no matter where one is placed.

I believe this ability is fundamentally linked to the level of one's consciousness. The lower the level of consciousness, the less the ability we have to uphold consistency between the abstract and the concrete. The higher the level of consciousness, the higher the level of awareness, and the higher the ability to work with unity.

## 3. I have never seen such a tiny lady with guts like a million elephants put together.

A third very fundamental characteristic of Dadi Janki is that she appreciates every question, every problem in the purest state of the origin of the question or problem. I have never seen her look down on a question, thinking it is too elementary. This has taught me that at the origins of existence there is something like a c-drive, the chip of the computer of our existence. In this place things do not have judgement, things are not good or bad. When questions are put to her that seem to me to be absolutely elementary, all of a sudden Dadi Janki grabs the question and brings it to this chip, and she gives it a spin that puts people into another realm. When

Dadi Janki talks, she touches the universal nature of everyone in the audience. This teaches us that there is unity in our spiritual lives that is real, from where all of us should be working.

I must say, also, that to do what she does and to be who she is in this world, you have to have a lot of 'guts', because you are going against the current. If all of us were like Dadi Janki, we would not be discussing many issues we confront today. I have never seen such a tiny lady going around like a nobody but with guts like a million elephants put together. There are no walls for her. One cannot be a transformational spiritual leader or teacher if you don't have guts. Spirituality is not a matter of living in a shelter.

## 4. The world of Dadi Janki is a world without frontiers.

This is something we all need to learn. We are born without frontiers but very soon afterwards we have all these walls to climb. Dadi Janki lives in a world with no boundaries.

I don't think her spiritual life was always this simple. The stories she tells me about her relationship with Brahma Baba (founder of the Brahma Kumaris) are tough ones. They were not just simple lessons she had to learn. There must have been huge work done on her part. So her lesson to me is: if you want to be good at it, you have to work at it. I don't think gifts come to you just the way you want them.

When people go to their offices, or to their homes, they see so many boundaries. You are black, she is white; you come from Africa, we come from Latin America; you are a Brahma Kumari, they are not; this is such a world of boundaries.

When Dadi Janki enters a room you know that she is walking in a world of no boundaries and we should ask ourselves, 'When are we going to get there?'

**5. It is an eternal puzzle for me to have met a woman who has no crisis of loyalty in life.**

Dadi Janki lives in a world without crisis of loyalty. It is so difficult to live in this world today with so many crises of loyalty. Loyalty to my family, loyalty to my institution, loyalty to this, that or the other. Every time one prepares a statement the tendency is to read it five to six times to see how to minimise a crisis of loyalty.

Our aim must be to live without crisis of loyalty. This aim is a major revolutionary experience, and also to some extent a frightening experience, because one would have to eliminate a number of things from one's life that we have given to ourselves as needed supports.

Where there is no crisis of loyalty, it is so simple to make a decision. You don't have to deal with so many differences of opinion, with who is going to say what and how. It is just so direct. You don't waste too much time in some railway station of life waiting for an answer. I have known very few people with this quality. Some leaders have a crisis of loyalty with money, some with their material existence, some with protecting their people.

We live in a world in which it is as if we are mesmerised into a need for some crisis of loyalty. Our value system is very penetrating and it creates so many new loyalties. Just look at television and advertising. Cigarettes, whiskies, perfumes, sexuality… You pay more because you have a crisis of loyalty. In this way the whole world is being manipulated. To find someone who has no crisis of loyalty at all, where the colour white is white and the colour black is black, and there is no grey judgement; this is amazing.

## 6. There is no compromise in the absolute.

Many people are struggling to understand what a living spiritual paradigm means. Dadi Janki represents a practical yardstick to measure whether you are in the spiritual paradigm or not.

She is always living in the absolute. You can see it in the priorities she has, in the topics she discourses on, in the way she guides people. There is nothing where you can say she is putting something down, or working in relative terms.

The way to the absolute is very simple. There may be many gates but the main gate that I have experienced is to become self-realised in the basic virtues of humanity. If you don't love, if you don't experience love in its totality; you cannot be in the absolute because the absolute is love. If you don't experience caring and sharing, you cannot be in the absolute because the absolute is caring and sharing by definition. If you are only interested in 'my' thing, e.g. 'my' salvation, 'my' enlightenment, you will never be enlightened because individual enlightenment is always connected to the collective. You could get close to 'the gate' but the Supreme will say: 'Where is your sister or brother? Where did you leave them?'

Dadi Janki loves the entire humanity. Of course, she has her own direction, because she has her own body, so she is aware of what she needs to do tomorrow morning - get dressed, eat, and talk to people. But she also has the plane of the totality.

The privilege of being with Dadi Janki is that this transformational power can actually help you go faster into this process. People like her are walking libraries of the absolute. We were all once in this state of the absolute and somehow we have lost it. How would we really know the difference if we didn't have someone whom we could see in the absolute?

## 7. Dadi Janki is the mirror you can look into and see your real face.

Someone asked me in relation to Dadi Janki: 'Does this stage of the absolute not result in a certain kind of inflexibility?' My answer is that one needs to transpose one's understanding of this reality. The question is: 'How clean do I want the mirror to be, to look at myself?' The cleaner the mirror, the clearer is my image.

She is the mirror to many souls, a point of reference. And this point of reference is her living in the absolute. You need to understand that somehow souls like her will transform others in relation to the absolute, not in relation to your own theories.

She does not force anyone to her scheme of the absolute. One cannot be her. One can learn from her existence, because all of us are different, and that is the beauty of it. We are not all equal in the spiritual realm as we are at different stages. In this lifetime you certainly have a choice, and that choice is either to have a clean mirror or not.

Dadi Janki teaches you to be the first person, spiritually.

## 8. Dadi Janki is invincible. She has no fear.

Dadi Janki has self-realised peace. She does not get into war with anyone. She is walking peace. Her beauty is to be in that state of the absolute. One does not come out of this state, as it is not a matter of choice any more. Once you reach the state of the absolute, everything changes.

To know is to have responsibility. To have spiritual knowledge is to embody a tremendous amount of responsibility, because in actual fact you know. Every reality already exists in ourselves. We are just finding ways to enliven them and to become them.

Not only are we responsible for how we wake up tomorrow morning, but by definition we are agents of change. So the question is not whether you are or you are not. The question is, what type of agent of change do you want to be?

It would be a privilege to attain Dadi Janki's level of the absolute: no crisis of loyalty, great transformational power, great precision and great purity of knowledge.

Inside*Out* offers us a unique guide to the ways of thinking and being that enabled Dadi Janki to reach such a goal. It is a mirror that shows us what we are and what we can become. It will help all of us move forward.

# Introduction

# Introduction

LIVE IN SUCH A WAY that love informs every action! I have learned to live this way, and as a result, nothing disturbs me. My contentment and good feelings towards others remain constant. I have become free.

The power that allows me to live like this comes from inside. I do not look for it from the outside. That is why I stay free, with no expectations of others, and no frustrations.

Everyone can live this way. It is a very natural way to be. However, it requires letting go of certain beliefs and habits that drain us of this strength, and interfere with our ability to love. Sometimes these have become deep-seated within us, such that we are not aware of their presence.

I am convinced there is now a fresh chance for us all. We are living in an era when those who turn their minds within, to the inner self and to God, can truly come together, in a new way. With courage and determination, we can access an ocean of peace, love, happiness and power that transforms the way we see ourselves and others.

The process of renewal is simple. Through time, cobwebs of illusion covered our eyes; now we need to be like the spider that swallows its own web. We need to gather in the threads of our old ways of thinking and feeling, recognising that these are no longer serving us as we had wished.

We thought we could find happiness outside of us, that we could live from outside to in. We succeeded up to a point, but our success eventually became self-defeating. It enabled us to dig an ever-deeper trap for ourselves. As long as our desires were satisfied, we felt encouraged to continue to look for satisfaction in an extroverted way.

This created a vicious circle. Well-being became more and more based on things outside of us, which are never stable. Consequently, insecurity and worry increased. We became trapped in a web of physical dependencies and addictions.

Then we became afraid, in case we should lose the things we had come to depend upon.

Finally, when we actually lost them, as happens sooner or later with everything physical, we suffered a lot internally.

Today, many find themselves imprisoned in worry, fear and sorrow because of such misunderstandings. It is as though the things of the outer world have been allowed inside, taking a hold where they don't belong, binding us to them and depriving us of our ability to be ourselves.

Suffering indicates the presence of misapprehensions of this kind. Experience has taught me that feelings such as sorrow, worry and fear are not original and natural to us. Such feelings arise when we let ourselves be influenced by beliefs and behaviours that do not belong to us. This in itself is a wonderful realisation. If suffering is not an intrinsic feature of human nature, then it can surely be removed. We can stop suffering, and help others to do the same.

Pain is different from suffering. Physical and emotional pain can serve as a useful signal, protecting us against harmful behaviours. We can learn from pain.

Suffering, by contrast, drains us of the power to interact accurately and constructively with the world around us. All too often, it has become a habit in itself. In fact, a major obstacle to our happiness is the belief that we have to suffer, as a natural and inevitable part of life.

Some people think God wants us to suffer. Others even talk about a suffering God. I see those as really damaging ideas. In fact, I feel that misunderstandings about God, with a resulting separation from God, underlie all our other impediments.

I have come to know God as a being of truth – a fountainhead of peace and love. My life has been built on learning to receive power from God. This brings an inner strength that is enormously valuable in life.

This is not a book about religion or philosophy as such, but I can't begin to address you without speaking of God.

Many in the world are weary of religion. Although the religious impulse is towards truth and wholeness, in practice it often turned into superstition and dogma. We tried to gain strength, but continued to lose it. The result was increased distrust, and fragmentation of the human family.

Science seemed to some to offer more hope, but it kept its focus almost exclusively on the material world and has done little to help strengthen us internally.

This book describes a means of escape. It's a question of turning within. When we learn how to focus the energy of our thoughts internally, and connect them to God, we become able to step free from these mental prisons.

By developing an inward focus to our lives, we develop the power to act in line with our true, positive nature. I feel sure that, deep down, it's how everyone wants to be: able to relate to the world with full generosity of spirit.

This different way of living brings a deep change in attitude and outlook. From being like a beggar in relationships with others, sometimes dependent and sometimes demanding, we become like a prince - not seeking to take, but able to give. From leading a life like a shell, brittle and insecure, we develop a powerful, diamond-like consciousness, immune to negative influence and suppression.

Even as a child I knew that this was how I wanted to live, but it was as a young woman - nearly 70 years ago - that I learned how to make it possible. Central to what I learned is a method for developing a relationship with God, based on peace, love and truth, and without fear.

With my mind, I have been practising and experiencing this relationship ever since. My life has been dedicated to refining this art, and sharing it with others.

As a result of the treasures I have received, people often feel, even at the sight of me, a long-forgotten memory of their own deepest truth stirring inside. When we meet, they experience a warmth and radiance which enables them to know what it means to be truly human.

Through having made God my companion, I am able to live completely from inside to out. This has taken me beyond everyday limits and constraints.

The aim of this book is to share the conviction that all can and will become the same – because this is truth. There is no need to think about it too much. That gets in the way of the experience.

There are five chapters, each examining one of five essential and original qualities, or attributes, that exist inside every one of us. These are: peace, love, purity, happiness, and the power of divine truth – a power that stems from deep self-realisation, and which is restored through the consciousness of being a child of God.

Our problem has been that whilst living in this body of five elements our mental energies gradually became trapped by our physical surroundings, including the body. We lost sight of our divinity. Consequently, those original qualities diminished. To the extent that we lost them, the gap tended to be filled by five negative tendencies, or vices: lust, anger, attachment, greed and ego.

These vices are not original to us, but they took more and more of a grip on our consciousness as our actions moved progressively further away from our true, original nature.

We lived increasingly from outside to in, such that the world outside eventually so dominated our thinking as to obscure or block our awareness of the inner being.

When I have the experience that I am, in truth, a divine being, distinct from the body, the original qualities of the soul re-emerge naturally. They become fully active again.

Living steeped in the awareness of my peace, love, purity and happiness, these qualities predominate in my being and shine forth, like a light. It is as though they create a subtle form for me, of light, and that this is how others will perceive and experience me.

That is divine power. It is what it means to become an angel.

The soul is still in a body, and the body may still carry negative predispositions arising from past actions, like shadows. But when I live with the consciousness of being a child of God, and of my own highest truth, it is as though I am living in light. Shadows disappear, and I radiate light. This is the form of an angel.

But that is the culmination of our journey.

The first task is to understand the enormous value of inner peace, what causes it to drain away, and how to begin to recover it and maintain it.

Chapter One

# The Power of Peace

PEOPLE NEED PEACE as much as they need food and shelter. Some have been searching desperately for peace, for a long time. It's missing in the lives of many. Worry, depression and exhaustion are at epidemic levels in prosperous countries, even when material needs are fully met.

I want to explain where peace comes from and how to harness and develop it. Peace is an energy created inside. Even when I speak with peace, and you listen with peace, the energy increases.

So many types of crisis take place in our lives. There may be upheaval in the body, or in relationships, or in the atmosphere of the world. I don't think that anywhere there is a person who has gone through life free from crisis - young, old, uneducated, wealthy.

But when I have the power of peace, I do not allow the stability of my mind to be disturbed. Stability of mind is essential to leading a good life.

Just think for a few moments: when a person is worried, fearful, or experiencing sorrow, what is his state? And how does it affect others?

If I allow myself to experience worry, fear or sorrow, I will make myself restless and unhappy and the atmosphere around me will be filled with similar feelings. How does that help either me or others?

In contrast, if I free the self from these negative emotions, I will find myself having good thoughts, filled with positive feelings towards others. This will help create a peaceful and loving atmosphere, even when harmony has been absent.

My experience tells me that when I am able to stay free from sorrow, fear and worry there are values in me that come to the fore and that will be used in my life practically, giving me much strength and power.

When there is physical illness, you may go to the doctor and be prescribed some medicine. But when you are experiencing sorrow in the mind, what will you say or do? What will your mind be like when you think negative thoughts? Whether this negativity is directed towards the self or others, the mind feels unhappy. Either way, such thoughts commit violence to the self.

Together with sorrow, there is also peacelessness. "I don't know what my mind is doing, it is chaotic." Yet it is your mind, and so why are you becoming unhappy about it? When you allow yourself to become peaceless, you will interact with others in the same way and you won't be able to speak sweetly or peacefully with them.

If there is no rain, human beings and animals become thirsty. If there is no peace or love in my mind, it is as though mind and heart are dry. The mind becomes restless and races like that of a crazy person. Even with sleeping pills, people in this condition can't sleep at night and then can't wake up in the morning.

Free yourself from the crisis that you create through your own negativity. There are so many external crises, you can't even count them. There is nothing you can do about that. But the crisis you create in your own mind, according to the quality of your thoughts – at least put a stop to that.

Your body, your wealth, your relationships and the world: all four bring a variety of situations in front of you. They don't ask your permission. They can change at any time and you can't prevent it.

One crisis hasn't finished and another begins. Natural calamities, earthquakes, floods, all come by themselves. They don't come as a result of someone calling them, nor do they go away to order.

But what is the condition of my mind, before the situation comes? When the mind is strong external difficulties stay external – they do not shake me inside and rob me of my stability. The mind stays peaceful, free from sorrow and worry.

When I have this strength, situations filled with sorrow can come but I won't feel sorrow inside. If a stone is thrown, it won't hit me. If someone insults me - no problem!

My head must remain cool and not instantly react. Not even reject. Let there be an acceptance of the scene. This acceptance makes me peaceful inside. Then my peaceful feelings alone will help the situation. Also, I'll know better what to do or what not to do.

To experience sorrow is an act of senselessness. Remember this very well. When you feel sorrow about something, understand that you are lacking some understanding. For whom should I feel sorrow? Does it help either me or others?

Internally, people do create many difficult situations for themselves. Arrogance, for example, makes you feel disrespect and causes you sorrow. Arrogance brings a desire for regard and respect and when you don't receive these, you feel it to be an insult. "Look, I do so much for them, but this is how they repay me." If I give from the heart, and don't have arrogance, I won't have such feelings.

If I have good virtues and my actions are good, my fortune will also be very good.

But to become upset, or to be unhappy about something, even to have an off-mood, is like putting a drop of poison into a pot of nectar. It spoils everything. It doesn't just take away peace, it brings unhappiness.

That is not why I am here! It is good if I can quickly make the atmosphere around me one of great happiness and joy.

# Letting go

Speaking for myself, I don't know how to tell jokes, but when I see someone crying, I won't leave that person until I see him or her smile. I don't need to do anything but give peace and love to that person. Internally, I feel it is just a tiny thing they are holding on to, causing them to go around with such a gloomy face. But they are making others worried or afraid, thinking about what is going on in that person's mind.

People feel sorrow when they are holding on to situations. They forget that these situations are external to them. All it takes is to let go. Once they achieve this, they become happy and peaceful again and can begin to smile. How often have we looked back on some previous trouble and wondered what all the fuss was about!

The art of living from inside to out is such that it not only enables us to let go of that which is outside of us, but builds such strength as to avoid being trapped by it in the first place.

When you too let go of things that are outside of you, and become free, you will begin to feel a state of stability filled with such happiness that no matter what happens you cannot lose it. Happiness has the powers of peace and love merged within it. Where there is peace and love you feel yourself to be a king. You have self-respect and feel yourself to be very strong, not someone who easily becomes upset and tearful like a baby.

You need to attend to the quality of the thoughts that you allow to come to mind. This is only sensible. It is, after all, your mind. Thoughts should be pure, elevated and determined. Then just see the results. Without rituals, postures, chanting, etc, you will experience peace of mind.

Ask your heart: Do I have pure, positive feelings for everyone, including myself? Am I paying attention to this, making it my priority as I move through life? Such feelings create an energy that automatically flows outwards, protecting you against negative influence.

If you do pay attention, you won't make mistakes. You won't feel sorrow, and you won't give others the opportunity to have thoughts about your state of sorrow. Otherwise, everyone else's attention will be drawn towards you, that this poor person is in difficulty, and you will feel low. That is no good for you, nor does it help others.

In my life, I have made a commitment: I will not feel sorrow or worry about anyone or anything. Nor will I allow anyone else to have such feelings for me. I will not be afraid of anyone nor will I make anyone afraid. I have to give co-operation with love, and help when help is required.

Even if someone else isn't giving me love, I don't have to spend anything in giving love to them. Others may not give me respect, but why should I let go of my virtue of giving respect? It is not good for me even to have the thought of not giving respect to someone who doesn't respect me, or who is an obstacle for me.

I am on a spiritual journey, and situations will definitely come. My duty is to continue driving in my own lane, and not obstruct others.

When travelling by plane, clouds come but at that point the pilot cannot ask why – he just knows he has to cross them. An announcement is made to fasten the seatbelt because of turbulence, but you don't have to create turbulence in yourself thinking the plane might crash. That is not sensible. With faith in the aircraft and the pilot, you stay peaceful and cooperative. Then the cabin crew stay happy with you, and you don't create an atmosphere of fear that might spread among the passengers.

With peace, with faith, create such a loving atmosphere that whatever comes, it will easily go away. This is the wisdom shown by the ancient storytellers when they wrote "And it came to pass…"

What gives this kind of stability? You must have seen a tower – to reach so high, it has a deep foundation. You need to become introverted, to go deep inside, and make yourself so strong that even if the whole world fluctuates, you remain stable.

This power comes from within, from your inner being. When your motives are pure and positive, and based on love and truth, there will be this power of peace.

Truth means much more than information which we may think, speak, read or write about. It means the power to remain silent and peaceful. Not even to think. Not to listen to a great deal, but to keep the essence of your being, your human qualities, in your intellect and awareness. To merge everything else that happens, inside or outside, as an ocean absorbs rivers, so that there is calm.

A state of truth is one in which whatever power you need for yourself and others to remain peaceful, that power is readily available at all times. I may be speaking, but even then I must remain peaceful inside. My breath, thoughts and time should be filled with peace and stability so that whoever comes in front of me finds me useful, and peace spreads everywhere. Then I am also useful to my own self.

It is not necessary to remember and speak about sorrowful things of the world that have happened in the past.

Equally, to spread news of whatever is happening in the world now in such a way as to cause fear and tension is unhelpful. If I become afraid, I won't be able to do anything useful.

# Turning within

Some people thought it was only by leaving their families and going to the jungles and the mountaintops that they'd be able to free themselves from worry and sorrow. But complete freedom doesn't lie that way. Rather, what one has to do is to be able to turn inwards. This spiritual endeavour is needed. The soul is trapped by its own body. It is trapped by its relationships. When one turns within, one is able to accumulate the spiritual energy with which to live in this world, free from fear.

In my own life I have never allowed myself to become afraid, but rather, I would help with the power of peace at times of difficulty. Many situations have come to me, some due to ill health or lack of finance, but I would not become confused, afraid or anxious.

I may not be educated (I only had three years of formal schooling), but I can at least remain peaceful and give peace to others. At least I can embrace someone with love.

When people are in fear, whom would they embrace? If they are caught up in worrying about what will happen to them and their children, what will they do for others? Such people are unable to take help from God, they are unable to help themselves and nor are they able to help the world. Free yourself from this kind of thinking.

The power to remain peaceful is accumulated through truthful actions performed with an elevated intellect – with understanding. To remain dependent on someone or to make someone dependent on you is the work of someone who is weak.

It is my duty to remain altruistic, and with honesty to remain harmonious and at one with others – to have a generous heart. Some people think of duty or responsibility as a burden. I become light! After all, what is my responsibility? To smile, to remain peaceful and to share these vibrations from my heart, through my attitude and my vision. Does anyone not have this responsibility?

I tell people: please don't change your face so often. Don't allow your face to look tired. It is good to remain tireless. Who can do this? Those who are internally strong, such that no matter what happens, it is not a big thing. Is this possible? Has your sorrow, fear and worry gone?

If you stay in a state of peace as you read this book, you'll understand the meaning of altruism and generosity. So please do read, but there's really no need to think! I want to make it easy for you by sharing things which you can absorb, but which you don't have to worry about. Just accept them, and let them filter into your heart.

People have the habit these days of thinking a lot. For everything useful, they say: "Well, I'll think about it." But when it is something useless, something that one shouldn't really do, they don't stop to think at all!

Allowing yourself to be unhappy is not useful. After you have finished reading this book, never say you are unhappy. Remember: sorrow is lack of understanding. Those who have negative thoughts have worry. Think good things and do good things. As you think, so your face becomes. Can you hide your thoughts from your face?

Why are you worrying? Do good, and it will turn out good. If you think good things, good things will happen. If you have doubts in advance, how can you expect good results?

Why are people unable to do good things? They make two mistakes. They remember things of the past, and they look at others to see how others are looking at them. Before doing anything, they are concerned about how others are seeing them.

Things of the past, and things of others, don't allow you to do good things. "This one is like this, and this one is like that" – such thoughts waste time and use up your energy. True peace and happiness create energy.

Critical and fearful thoughts concerning others come from lack of self-respect. Those who have fear of others have fear about themselves, and become nervous. There isn't strength inside.

I don't become nervous. Why should you? Become so strong that nothing matters. Then even those who come to shake you become strong.

It is very simple. Become so strong, that no matter what is thrown at you, you won't collapse. Spiritual bombs of peace are much more powerful even than the atom bomb. We have all the good material to prepare such bombs, secretly.

If only 100,000 people prepare such bombs of peace, they will create such beautiful vibrations that everyone will forget their worry and fear, and faces will begin to blossom.

You worry about the children. You worry about the old people. Don't worry about anyone, but become like the fire brigade that comes at the time of a fire to put it out. Become part of such a real army, a powerful army.

Take the initiative in this, and it will happen. If you wait for others to do something and only then consider doing it, you will never do it. Don't look at others! Adopt the attitude: "I have to do this. I have to do it now. I am very clear about what I have to do. All my focus is on this. Let me do, such that I am useful to God and to others. Otherwise, why am I living this life?"

When I am with that One, even I alone will be powerful. No one can then do anything to me. This is real, powerful peace, not the temporary peace that comes through avoiding difficult situations, or suppressing feelings.

Mercy, honesty, love and peace in my life should give life to others.

These qualities come unlimitedly from God. They are working on me and they should work on others. With the power of experience, care for others and share with others according to the time, and inspire others through your life. This is also to have real mercy for the self.

To be like this, I cannot afford to have any wasteful or negative thoughts. If such thoughts emerge, I sweep them away like ants. If there isn't peace of mind, there is weakness inside. When somebody has peace internally, they are very strong.

I have to talk to myself in a very mature way. In my own life, if someone in my connection is doing something wasteful despite my good wishes for them, I tell myself: OK, I must continue to give good wishes and not look at what they are doing. I cannot tell them, "Don't do this, do that", or even think that way. I have to think to myself, "Everything will work out fine." It helps much more to keep myself merciful, loving and peaceful in this way than to become upset.

I only think about things that I have to do. Some activities are natural, and don't take any thought at all. I will accumulate peace and happiness through them, so why should I have any thoughts about them? Success lies in that which brings me peace, power and happiness. That is real work!

Chapter Two

# The Power of Love

THOUGHTS AND FEELINGS of worry, fear and sorrow are no use to us. They weaken us, and cannot help us find lasting solutions to our problems. In a sense, they are the problems. If I have the strength to respond to a situation with calm and ease, it is no longer a problem.

But then the question arises, how can we rid ourselves of such thoughts and feelings? Are they not part of the human condition? How can we maintain positive feelings when so much is wrong with the world – including ourselves?

It is true that when we are weak, we can't do anything about such feelings. They take us over. However, although weakness may be widespread, it is not our natural condition.

Originally, each of us is naturally powerful. Power in this inner context means something akin to the French expression, *joie de vivre*. It means being well stocked with the energy of positive thought and feeling, and knowing how to use and maintain those stocks effectively, replenishing them from an inner wellspring. In this powerful state you feel love for the self, for others, for life.

When you begin to think positively, you accumulate power. Your self-confidence and effectiveness increase. When you allow negative thoughts to come, it is as if a leak develops in the vessel of the soul.

Even moments of negativity, such as casting a critical eye towards another, automatically cause a loss. You cannot be both positive and negative at the same time. If you slip into prolonged bouts of doubt and criticism, concerning either the self or others, you'll become drained of all the strength you have inside. Such thoughts and feelings take you into a state of turmoil, confusion, and eventually depression. You'll have no idea of what you are supposed to do or how to do it. You'll feel like a stranger in this world, friendless and purposeless.

However, a point comes when you realise: "What is this way of thinking and feeling doing to me, and to my attitude and vision towards others? It's destroying me." This can be a painful realisation, but experience shows that it is the first step towards regaining power.

You realise that you have to make yourself rise above not just negative thoughts, but wasteful and ordinary thoughts too. The reason is that all such thoughts disturb your inner peace, and inner peace is needed in order to be able to draw energy and accumulate power from God.

When the surface of a lake is disturbed it can no longer reflect the surrounding hills or sky. Try to look into it, and you won't get past the ripples or waves. The water will seem murky. But when it is still, you can see into its depths, and with a slight shift of focus you can also see beauty reflected from above.

It is the same with the self. Before you can develop love for or even a deep interest in the inner self and God, you need to look at the quality of your thoughts. You have to make them peaceful and pure, even if only temporarily.

The process of realising the true nature of the self and God can also be compared to lighting a lamp. You need a clean wick, protection against the wind, and a little oil. Once the flame is lit, the lamp burns by itself, drawing on the reservoir of fuel.

The wick is your inner cleanliness. Your thoughts and feelings need to be clean. For this, it is essential to distance yourself from past hurts and resentments, at least long enough to get the lamp going. Worries and desires for the future also have to be left on one side.

Similarly, consciously choose not to think about others for a while. Comparisons, jealousy and criticism create emotional storms that also make it difficult to light the lamp. Instead, remember what it means to be still, self-contained, in the present, beyond conflict and confusion.

Then draw on positive thoughts and feelings such as peace, happiness, acceptance, and kindness. The experience of such qualities is the oil that primes the lamp. It creates a link with God. The reason is that we share these qualities with God.

When you have made these preparations, all that remains is to kindle the light inside with a spark of love. This can come automatically, when you have narrowed the gap between God and yourself.

Then the energy flows. This an amazing, wonderful thing. It is all that is missing in our lives. It is this energy of love that makes it possible to live from inside to out – to become a beacon, in fact - and to prevent the negativities that exist outside from coming in, draining us of happiness and strength.

You feel that God is with you, that He is your companion, and that you have all the love and understanding you need. It's as if within the flame there is the fuel that makes the light shine brightly. It shows in your eyes, on your face, and it comes through in your actions. It lightens up others, too.

The feeling is a completely natural one. I don't see it as either supernatural or mystical. It has to do with what some scientists call the energy of pure consciousness. But there is magic in the way it transforms.

## Source of living energy

There is great happiness in understanding that this source of living energy is available to us. It is distinct from us – that is why the current flows - but our own human nature is such as to be able to receive and distribute this energy from God.

We can see it working at three different levels, or degrees of intensity, within the self, corresponding to three stages of the journey back to our truth.

The first level comes with remembering God, which means taking steps of love towards God. It's a return journey. God is not really such a big mystery. We have known Him, but forgotten Him.

The second level is associated with relationship with God, which develops as I practise the experience of a concentrated, non-physical awareness and state of mind known as soul-consciousness. I can begin to see the energy of God's love working in my life.

The third level comes when there is deep connection with God. It brings completion within the soul, and power.

As human beings we have the unique faculty of an intellect, which allows us to make deliberate choices about how to direct our thoughts and feelings, sending them in a particular direction.

Many do feel they would like to remember God. However, they are frustrated in that aim because mind and intellect are caught up elsewhere. The intellect has developed the habit of remembering all sorts of physical attractions and concerns. It has allowed the mind to enter into such deep relationship and connection with aspects of the physical world as to become trapped by them.

This is the root cause of our problems. The physical world itself is not the problem. It is like a beautiful stage, on which the drama of life is enacted.

It is when we become over-absorbed and lose ourselves in the scenes and roles of this drama, forgetting that we are actors on the stage, that we become distanced from our inner truth.

We have to gently teach the mind and intellect to stop wandering around outside, looking to material aspects of existence for a sense of purpose and direction. We have developed the habit of taking comfort and support from these aspects, forgetting they can only ever be temporary since the whole of the material world is in a constant state of flux.

Sometimes it is "my" possessions, or "my" body, that have taken a grip on me in this way. When that is the case, a loss of wealth or health will distress me far more than when my sense of who I am is rooted at a deeper level.

Or perhaps I have a feeling of ownership towards another human being or human beings. It could be "my" partner, "my" relatives, "my" friend or even "my" enemy. Or I may have become absorbed by "my" position in the world.

Thinking too strongly in this "my" and "mine" way, it is as if I am trying to bind myself and this world outside of me together, in order to control it. In all such cases, I am setting myself up to suffer, because actually, when I do this, I am handing over my freedom.

I lose sight of the real self, which is the inner being, and of God, the One whom I really can call mine eternally. I lose my energy, my power, and ultimately my self-respect.

As long as my consciousness is trapped by the body and its physical relationships and connections, I can't experience the freedom and happiness that are rightfully mine. Consequently, I can't fulfil my responsibilities in my relationships with others, either.

The secret of living from inside to out is to get to know ourselves again internally, and recover an ability to draw on the energy of our inner truth. Then, we can be free!

Why are young children often so loveable? We love the uncritical, innocent pleasure we see in them, when they are free from material worries and the fear and sorrow that go with those worries. While that innocence lasts, they don't have concerns about their body, or their role in life. They just get on with living.

The light in the eyes of a child steeped in the love of life and the joy of the moment reminds us of our own original condition of freedom.

Remembering that originally I too am a free spirit is the key to becoming free, that I can draw on an unlimited source of love, wisdom and happiness when I stop looking for these qualities in the world outside, and instead attend to my inner world.

I have to realise the importance of this deliberate act of remembering, and learn to use my intellect to practise and develop a taste for turning my thoughts away from the outside world, and going within.

You remember someone or something when it has become distanced from you. Near or far, it is as though your mind or consciousness travels to that person or object, so that relationship and connection can be renewed. However, you need to focus in order to do this, which means putting aside other pulls on your intellect.

It is the same with remembering God. To move accurately in God's direction, I have first to take my thoughts beyond this physical world. There is a saying in India: you can't put two swords in one sheath.

So, turning within, I withdraw my thoughts from the outside world, including the body, and focus on my inner, spiritual identity. I think of this essence of the self as being like a point or star, dimensionless in terms of time and space, but situated behind the eyes, a centre of awareness. This has been remembered in some spiritual traditions as the third eye.

Opening the third eye is like opening a window on to another world. Whilst still here in the body, I am able to take my thoughts far beyond, even beyond the physical universe. I feel a sense of transcendence of material reality, and of entering a realm of peace. I understand this realm to be my original home, and also God's home.

I think of God as also being like a point or star, dimensionless, but radiant with the power of truth, unlimited and eternal.

As my consciousness reaches this incorporeal awareness and stage, it then becomes possible to develop a relationship with God. This takes me to a higher level of energy inside. Every time I remember God, the relationship deepens. It's such a beautiful discovery, that I can visit the Supreme Soul whenever I want, internally.

When you have a good relationship with someone, you receive cooperation from them. When I leave to one side all my worldly relationships and connections, I experience all God's qualities and powers. I recharge, filling with this energy of truth that is also my own truth.

When I return to my responsibilities in the physical world after recharging in this way, I find I can easily and naturally keep a positive frame of mind. Because of the strength I have taken into myself, my actions have a positive power about them that is a pleasure to express, and which also benefits others.

When something is false, it often has a superficial attraction. We fall in love with so many false things. Even our everyday interactions are often full of falsehood, insofar as there is a hidden selfishness present.

Because of ego, for example, we work for praise and position, instead of from a sense of service. Because of attachment or desire, we try to control others, or allow them to control us, often whilst portraying these feelings and behaviours as signs of love.

We deceive ourselves, as well as the people we interact with, so much. This is why so many relationships run into difficulties.

To escape all this, there has to be the aim that I don't want any falsehood to remain in my life. I want to see an end to any kind of deceit in myself, or in my interactions with others. All untruth, with myself and with others, has to go.

As my relationship with God deepens, its value to me increases and it becomes a real, living connection. I begin to understand what true love really means, as a state of being rather than a desire. Feeling the joy and strength of this love, I see clearly the contrast with ego and attachment. I realise the difference between truth and falsehood. The only deep desire remaining in me is the desire to become completely truthful inside, to attain truth. This burns like a flame inside me.

As this flame intensifies, it purifies the soul, removing negative tendencies. Relationship and connection with God do the work. It is as if God acts like a goldsmith, removing alloy from the soul. In time, the only thoughts that come are pure and beneficial ones - thoughts of love, peace, mercy and compassion.

So, I find myself living in the same body, with the same wealth and relationships, and in the same world. But inside, because the thoughts have become pure gold, there is now love and truth radiating out to all.

There is a final step, in which the connection between me and God becomes like a blood relationship, so deep as to be unbreakable. When this happens, the energy I receive gives me such strength that not only has falsehood been removed from inside me, but the falsehood that exists outside can't enter me and influence me any more.

Even beyond pure gold, the soul can be seen as a beautiful, tiny diamond inside. When there is the deepest connection with God, you realise and recognise yourself as this jewel. Outside, there is a body. There is wealth. There are relationships. There is this world. But who am I? The sparkling, spiritual jewel.

As I come closer and closer to God, it is as if the Supreme, like a jeweller, guides me into seeing what flaws remain, and how to remove them. There is a flow of very subtle but powerful communication. The love I receive from God is like light, filling me with true self-respect and self-realisation, displacing the flaws created by ego.

The goal then is to be a flawless jewel, set in the pure gold of my original qualities and nature, radiating the purest thoughts and feelings, absolutely valuable.

# Everything the soul needs is in God

Somebody once asked me, how much meditation do you do? I replied, when you really love someone, and in your heart you feel you are receiving unlimited benefit from them, you just don't want to stop taking. You feel they are inseparable and that you are with them all the time.

There is that much power in God's love. It's so beautiful. It is truth – it reveals the original quality of the soul. It finishes even a trace of impurity. The fire of that love burns in such a way that all the rubbish inside dissolves, until nothing but truth remains.

It was when I realised the contrast between truth and falsehood that I was able to bring about transformation in myself. I saw the beauty of God's truth first in India, in the mid-1930s. It was present in Prajapita Brahma, founder of the spiritual university to which I have given my life.

Having filled myself with God's love and wisdom, I find that others are helped to realise the contrast when they see this truth in me. Often, it serves as an inspiration for change.

The mind is always drawn to and will settle on a place in which there is a deep sense of belonging, and of attainment; and this is what the mind experiences in its connection with God.

Everybody wants to feel that sense of belonging. Even household pets really want their owners to love and appreciate them. A dog will then protect such a household, not letting strangers inside.

The soul deeply needs a sense of belonging. It finds it in God when it is reminded of its own eternal nature of peace, love, power, purity and happiness, and through that, remembers God and rediscovers all that God can do.

Everything the soul needs is in God. That includes all relationships – mother, father, teacher, friend, guide, beloved. When God becomes the focus of the soul's life, the soul finds that deep sense of belonging, of peace, of having found its home. Within that, it receives truth and love. And that truth and love bring power.

Whatever happens inside someone, comes out in their life. So, although I, as the soul inside, am distinct from the brain and body, nevertheless, whatever is going on inside me will have an impact on the body and come out in my actions and interactions.

Whatever the thoughts, whatever the feelings, so will be my attitude towards life and my vision towards others.

When I think in a pure, peaceful way, I can progress to thinking about God. There is then that flow of love, and bliss, through connection with God. Understanding God also brings me a lot of wisdom internally.

The feeling comes that I didn't have this previously – this peace, love, happiness, truth; I'd lost those qualities. Now they are re-emerging inside me. So I, the soul, am the first to benefit. But because my attitude towards others and also my vision towards them – the way I see them and connect with them – are now governed by these qualities, there is benefit all round.

Generally, it seems that human beings have become very dependent. It's as if they can't even stand on their own two feet but are constantly bowing down, on all fours, like animals. It is a pitiful state of being. Being on the floor like that, they don't have their hands free to give, but they must take.

So often, even the food that people eat comes through dishonest means, in which they are exploiting other people, or animals, or nature, rather than earning it honestly.

Imagine the consequences, if a human being changes from a state of dependency like that and instead becomes truthful, honest, upright, and earning a living with integrity.

Not only does he then feed himself with that honesty, but he has enough to share with others. Just think what a different world it would be if we were to change in that way.

So, when I realise that I am a child of God, that God is accessible to me as my spiritual Mother and Father, and that I can draw unlimited love and truth into myself through connection with this wonderful parent, with such an understanding it's as if I begin to realise what it really means to be a human being.

I can stand on my own two feet again, and with that, my sense of being truly human comes back. I let go of ego, and attachment.

Because of the happiness I feel inside, I stop taking (and giving) sorrow. Even if someone throws something at me, I easily deflect it. So there is no need for feelings of retaliation or revenge.

# The consciousness of an angel

As my thinking and perception change in this way and my intellect begins to become elevated and wise, the pure desire grows inside that everyone should benefit from the understanding God is giving.

Then it's as if I take myself far above, and the intellect is only aware of one thing: I, the soul, am a child of God, and as a child of God I only want to give happiness. I want to see an end to the sorrow of the world below.

It's almost as if I don't have to do anything physically to bring that benefit, but there are such elevated, loving feelings in the heart that those feelings do the work from above...I just raise a hand of blessings, as it were, and that moves things.

When there is divinity in my interactions, it's as if I am operating at a level beyond matter. I am here, but I am also far, far above and beyond.

In my dealings with others, I am beyond any consciousness of colour, creed, riches or poverty, sickness or health. It is as though I am not interacting with human beings, but with divine or subtle beings – with the actor, not the physical costume or role.

When I am in this consciousness of my own divinity, and the divinity of others, it means that I am able to be a constant bestower. Whoever comes in front of me can just take, take and take and I'll continue to give and give and there will be the feeling inside, "Yes, by all means, just take what you want."

Divine beings like that are angels. They never count how much they have given. There's no question of counting because it's not coming from them. There's just a constant flow coming through them, from above, from God. They have the feeling that God is giving… just let that flow continue. There is just that sharing, and the feeling inside the heart, "Let people take as much as they can, let them fill themselves, it's the unlimited Bestower who is giving."

Angels have been remembered as circling in the sky above, at dusk, bringing protection and help as the day comes to a close. This is the feeling that people of this world should now have, that somewhere out there, angels are flying around and looking down and they are there for us, they are protecting us, they are there! We have these angels over us, giving us love, giving us power, giving us protection.

People of the world are beginning to see that those whom they considered to belong to them, and to be their support and help, are letting them down. Everything seems to be falling apart down here. And so of course worry, fear and sorrow are increasing inside.

But the angels up above should draw attention away from such feelings, towards God. There should be such a feeling of love and mercy and compassion from above as to be like a call inside, reaching down to the Earth.

When people hear this call, their eyes will be drawn upwards, to the sky, and they will feel: "There's someone out there for me...there are some divine beings, sending me good feelings and good wishes, protecting me...I can feel them, up above, within reach...they are there for me."

So, even if people can't go as far as connecting with God, at least let them have this feeling of belonging and protection from angels, who are not too far away.

Just as science and technology are able to make signals travel very far, whether through sound or vision, it's a law that whatever is inside consciousness also comes outside. Whatever is in people's eyes and hearts will reach others.

If there is that subtle, angelic feeling and presence, people's hearts will be touched and drawn up above. Those subtle vibrations will reach and draw others, no matter what part of the world they are in.

People won't have to listen to the radio or watch the television to obtain what they need. They'll go inside, and they'll be able to pull that vibration – that energy of truth – from above. They may not even need to pull it. It may just come to them, at the time of need, as a shower brings coolness and freshness on a hot summer's day.

We have to be like clouds, filled with love, truth and purity, showering on the people of the world. There is great power for change in this.

Ask yourself: "Who am I, after all? Who do I belong to? And what are God, time and my own internal voice telling me to do? Am I responding to that?" And actually, in that going inside, it's as though you are automatically carried above the world, away from your worries and fears, such that the power of love and truth you receive can then bring comfort to many others.

Chapter Three

# The Power of Purity

I DRAW LOVE AND POWER into myself through relationship and connection with the Supreme. I make that love and power my own so that it constantly radiates into the world. This is the royal path to real, lasting peace.

It is as though God, who is truth, gives me the aim of making my life truthful and valuable, like a diamond. As I move towards this goal, my thoughts and feelings become very light. I feel like a free spirit, still part of this world but not bound by it. I can fly, like an angel, in the service of humanity.

Before there can be such complete truth in my life, there has to be purity. Purity underpins the entire process of restoring truth into my character and relationships.

Purity enables me to make my thoughts and actions free from the negativity, waste and weakness that were created when I ceased to understand myself as a spiritual being, and thought of myself only as the offspring of my physical parents and circumstances.

God shows me real, true, love, and, through that, teaches me to understand the difference between truth and falsehood. This creates an inner light and warmth, a rekindling of the flame of the soul, that forms the heart of the process of purification. Care is needed to keep the flame burning strongly and complete the job of becoming free.

Purity and truth are different states. Purity means free from impurities. Truth means whole, without deception or falsehood.

I wouldn't say a glass of water was true, for example, but I would want it to be pure. It would then be good to drink and would help to keep the body healthy, functioning true to its purpose; in other words, fulfilling its potential.

When thought is pure, it enables my life to be truthful and valuable and my potential as a human being to be fulfilled. Purity clears a path for truth. It makes space inside my mind in which truth can be experienced.

In fact, originally the soul is truth, so when I clean my mind of thoughts and desires that cause disturbance I can begin to comprehend and recognise what truth is and appreciate its value in my life.

Purity within the soul is essential for peace. When purity is lacking in even the slightest way, there cannot be peace.

Love, too, cannot remain true and honest if physical desires are mixed in with it.

Some people think they have peace in their lives, and others that they have love. But if purity is not there as well, there can't be contentment.

You may be experiencing peace through having moved away from your responsibilities. Or people may be giving you love just to keep you happy. As long as there is some weakness mixed inside, however, you can't really experience peace or happiness. Your love will not be constant, either. Sometimes you'll stay loving, and sometimes you'll not even be capable of giving love to yourself.

When I embrace purity in my life, it serves to finish all traces of the physical from my thinking. A human being has a body, of course, but the point of purity is to become free from the hold that the body has on my consciousness. This is what makes it possible for me to live and serve as an angel.

When someone really understands this, and puts it into practice in their life with honesty and the power of truth, that is wisdom.

Purity comes through relationship and connection with God. Without the power of this connection, there cannot be complete purity.

The renunciates of India, who follow celibacy, do so with great difficulty. They leave their homes, hide in caves, and suffer dietary and other privations.

But God injects purity deep into the soul. Actually, what this relationship really does is to give an injection that extracts the impurity that has infiltrated the soul. The soul is truth, and so with purity you are able to experience that truth.

God gives us knowledge of our original state of purity, but the knowledge is not just for the intellect. It is not just information; it is a deep and beautiful experience. When you make this connection, you are able to taste the sweetness of real love, like nectar. This sweetness draws out the poison.

Then there's the feeling of new blood being inside the soul. It is as though you awaken. You become aware of what is real within you and around you. Peace comes. The heart feels so comforted.

For a long time, it hasn't been in human consciousness that it is possible to experience such peace, love and happiness – such reality. The peace, love and happiness that come as a result of purity are filled with truth.

It is said that information is power. In a limited sense, that may be true. When we can access information about how things work, they become useful to us.

But spiritual knowledge requires much, much more than information. To have the power to absorb it and use it, we need purity.

The essence of spiritual knowledge is very simple. It is to know who we really are, as souls that our original home, the ground of our being (as opposed to our doing), is non-material, and that this home is also where we connect with the Supreme Soul.

But without inner purity, the connection is weak and therefore power does not accumulate. So, it is essential to give ourselves time to really understand what purity is.

## Restoring the connection

God, the Supreme, makes us aware of the truth and beauty He contains. In connection with Him, we understand that this is what we were too, that this is our truth, and the process of becoming that again begins. He says to us: "Hey souls, see the original Father. Recognise Me. See how I am. I am the Purifier."

When you absorb this knowledge and awareness inside, it's like digesting food. When you eat, blood made from the food goes into your veins to give strength and power inside. When you take the right things into yourself spiritually - the right understanding, the right practice, the nectar of relationship and connection - and turn these into new blood, all the rubbish is extracted. Then there is purity.

Absorb so much of this energy within yourself that the soul becomes pure, the body becomes pure, and those who come in front of you become pure. It is possible to have that much power.

The body reflects the state of your consciousness. When you make yourself a slave to its appetites and addictions, a vicious cycle develops in which those appetites increase. When you take God's energy into yourself, the senses become cool. The body loosens its hold on you. You regain mastery.

It is said that only a golden vessel is fit to contain the milk of a lioness. Anything less, and the milk turns sour. Even ordinary milk quickly goes off if it is put in an inappropriate container.

In the same way, the true peace of God, the peace and understanding that taste so sweet, that give so much strength and wisdom, will only stay within where there is purity. Purity makes your mind and intellect like gold.

It's not just peace of mind that is needed, or peace within your mind. It's the strength that comes from having attained victory over the impurities which destroyed your peace.

There needs to be the certainty and conviction, "I've done it!" Within that victory, there is the power to adopt truth even to the point of not remembering that the impurities existed. They become literally unthinkable. There is no place for them in you any more.

Then you are immune to outside influence. Nothing can erode your peace and love. Self-respect fully returns, and you become fearless and free from animosity. You are not worried, angry or defensive about someone else's weakness.

Only purity gives such imperishable peace. When there is purity your peace will never be disturbed. Never! Purity enables peace to sit inside you, to become at home inside you. Then what you give out becomes naturally loving and peaceful, filled with the quality of purity.

Purity gives you a big, merciful heart. It keeps you enthusiastic, with the strong feeling inside that everyone should benefit from God's truth. Purity enables you to recognise truth, and adopt it, and donate it.

When truth completely fills you, falsehood has no place to stay in you any more. God is truth, and when you feel and experience this truth within yourself, the consciousness of everything else finishes. It doesn't matter how much ego or arrogance there may have been, that negativity disappears.

You stay connected to God, and your actions are good. It is as though God's power can work through you and fulfil beneficial tasks through you. The more that happens, the more powerful you become, too.

Purity itself is filled with elevated, beneficial feelings. The result is love: the feeling inside that others should have these same liberating experiences. This is real, spiritual love. Not the love that some people speak about which is really just an offer of entertainment, a laugh, a diversion.

If there is the slightest impurity inside, that is when worry, fear and sorrow can sneak in, so that you are adding to the world's problems rather than resolving them. In contrast, the love that comes from purity and peace increases your capacity to work altruistically, and the feeling of wanting others to benefit in a true way creates an elevated atmosphere that subtly supports others.

The true One makes you pure – really, solidly, pure. The serenity visible on the face of someone like that is amazing. It's peace that can finish other people's peacelessness just by seeing it.

So – purity first!

# How to regain purity

Purity means to have cleanliness inside the temple of the mind. In my own life, every day, I spend time examining myself internally to make sure no rubbish has slipped inside. This is part of my regular meditation. If I see anything negative, hidden away somewhere, I clear it out. When the temple is clean, God will come and sit in it. Then there is the power inside that stops any more rubbish from entering.

Purity brings out honesty. It prevents my relationship with God from being casual or careless. When I have that clear determination to be clean inside, I pay attention to making sure that I keep my thoughts and feelings positive. I don't let them create new stains inside.

Sometimes people expect God to love them, and then if they experience God's love they give love and remembrance in return. But you can't make conditions like that. If you want God's love, you also have to do something for God; you have to play your part in staying clean. There has to be a pure, clean love between you and God – not a bargaining or compromise.

Purity gives birth to truth. When you maintain inner cleanliness, your heart stays true to God and your actions come from that place of truth. Then you'll experience real peace, love, happiness and power.

When there is total purity, you will develop trust, honesty and integrity in relationships. With such a life, there is no room for worry, fear or sorrow. Purity makes you completely peaceful inside.

Purity gives the recognition of how valuable truth is. Then, when rubbish does come inside, you are readily able to recognise it and remove it. When this habit of maintaining inner cleanliness is firmly established, it's as if God's help is always close at hand.

Sometimes, when the mind is peaceless, I deliberately invoke thoughts of the soul and God, and a pure and peaceful state of mind returns.

At other times, purity won't come so readily. I may be trying to move into the consciousness of the soul, and to separate from the consciousness of the body, but just can't do it. Then, all of a sudden, I have the thought of the true Father and awareness of the Father's love – and my own true self-awareness and peace of mind is automatically restored.

If I have developed a love for this inner truth, and the habit of remembering the true Father, it's as if the Father reaches out to me when my own strength has failed.

Love for God creates a purifying fire inside. Different levels of intensity of this heat accompany different phases of purification.

The first level of attention is on removing layers of old things from the past, as when a decorator burns paint off a door.

When I make the effort to become clean in that way, the purity that is within shines through. That purity then reminds me of the value of having a clean, simple life, and of becoming honest.

When there is purity inside, I'll have the feeling of not wanting to tolerate any form of dishonesty in myself, whether in the form of carelessness, laziness, or making excuses. If I have laziness inside, that will lead me to make excuses, which means I am not being honest.

I need truth in all aspects. There is truth in making honest, sincere effort, with a true and honest heart. This is different from truth in the sense of an original state of being, such as when gold is pure, or when a painting or a piece of furniture is restored.

But the two are linked. To recover my truth, I need to make true efforts; and to make true efforts, I need a vision of my own original, true state of being.

I need to remember God with a heart that is honest and true. For that, I need at least to be clean enough inside to know what truth looks like – the original, positive, state of the human being, before it acquires the layers of dirt and dust that obscure the inner reality. This realisation equips me with elevated intentions and pure feelings, such that I really want to do this.

When I serve others, it is also with a true heart, absolutely sincerely. When I give someone my time, I give it to them with my heart, not just superficially or with a thought of finishing with them.

Similarly, if I give time to myself, let me do that also with great love and sincerity, from my heart. That's truthful. I need this truth in my effort in order to become pure.

When no trace of impurity remains, and there is no mixture of any sort in my motives, such purity gives me a wonderful feeling of truth. This fuels the fire of love. Deep interest develops in maintaining this experience, so that it becomes more concentrated and intense.

This is the second stage of purification, that of becoming true, real gold, with the alloy that had entered me removed.

The first level of purity is valuable and necessary, but is such that it can still be spoilt sometimes. According to the atmosphere or company, rubbish can enter my mind and create a storm of fear, anger or sorrow.

But when I become real gold, it means I am so full of truth as to have left falsehood far, far behind.

Even gold is not the highest destination. Gold is warm, beautiful, and valuable but it is also soft. This quality makes it easy to mould, but can also make it vulnerable to being dented or scratched.

Thus, when it comes to feelings, even a personality of pure gold is not immune to being hurt. And if I am hurt, I am still not in a state of truth.

The ultimate in purity is to develop a diamond intellect. In such a state, it is as though the intellect is so filled with truth that it sees everything, perceiving and recognising the truth of every situation; whilst also seeing nothing, in that it allows nothing to detract in the slightest from the truth within.

A perfect diamond is so strong that nothing ordinary can scratch it. It is also so multi-faceted and radiant that light comes from it in every direction. It is so valuable that everyone wants to see it; and yet (in the case of the greatest of all diamonds) so priceless that nobody can own it.

A diamond intellect, set within a golden personality, prepares the soul to become a deity – living in a body, but in a state of such perfection as to reveal God's qualities in human form.

## Love and wisdom

How can I reach such a stage? The experience of love for God, and of God's love for me, turns my thoughts and feelings into pure gold - rich, full, desireless, a mind that shines with truth. And God's knowledge makes me a diamond. The two work hand in hand.

In spirituality, God fills the soul with pure, real love and this finishes any trace of impurity, freeing me completely. In contrast, the love I received from human beings was so often deceitful. It finished my energy.

Purity then enables the sun of knowledge to rise inside me. When I keep that light with me, it shines out like a third eye, showing me what is truth and what is falsehood. In this jewel-like awareness, the light of the soul - the energy of consciousness - falls on that which is true and virtuous rather than false. I develop an intellect like a swan, which is said in folklore to have such power of discrimination as to pick up only jewels, ignoring stones.

When the light of the soul is kept focused on virtue in this way, seeing past falsehood, it reflects back to me in the form of love and appreciation and blessings from others. Truth multiplies inside me. The drains on my energy are stopped.

Knowledge means light; ignorance means darkness. If I don't have knowledge about something, I can't act appropriately – I am in the dark. When the sun rises, the darkness is dispelled automatically. The impurity that made me ignorant, and a slave to my own desires and the desires of others, finishes.

When there is ignorance it is as if I am blind, with an intellect like a stone. If you are blind, it is difficult to do anything, even if there is light all around.

Knowledge in the spiritual context means to know the truth about the soul. The impurities that used to cover that truth made me ignorant about the self and others. The sun of knowledge burns away those impurities and reveals the truth to me. It shows me the harm that I did to myself in allowing my consciousness to be trapped by the material world, and the joy and power that I receive when I learn to connect again to God.

The ways of thinking that I acquired from the world outside deceived me a lot. I was pushed this way and that, according to how the body wanted me to move, how others in my connection wanted me to move, and how the world wanted me to move.

The knowledge that comes from deep inside, from God, teaches me that although I am in this body, and through the body I have a connection with other people and the physical world, I am separate from all of that. I am a being of conscious energy, distinct from matter.

I must continue my connection with the material world, because that is how life expresses itself; but I'm not going to do things under the influence of all those outside factors any more. Because I am separate, I can choose. I can be the master. This is wisdom.

Old or young, when I have knowledge of the true self I can become truthful and wise. This also enables me to become sensible and mature.

When I am approaching life from the standpoint of ego, with my sense of who I am tied up with the body and its relations and connections with the world, I am over-sensitive about what goes on around me, getting upset over small things all the time like a small child. With the understanding that comes with purity, I don't get disturbed. This saves an enormous amount of energy.

Ignorance not only blinds me but may make me excessively forceful in my character, so that I try to influence and control others. I don't realise that I am doing wrong, nor that I am making others around me do wrong as well.

For someone who is in the dark in this way, money and position are everything, whereas those who have light inside know that if they have God with them, they also have their self-respect, which means they have everything.

Imagine a personality like this. Sensible, wise, cheerful; never doing anything just to show off to others. And never looking at the mistakes of others, either. That's a waste of time and thought. Such a one will feel, what have I got this invaluable knowledge for, if not to stay free?

The inner eye is such that it sees things as they are, for what they are. The knowledge that comes with purity means to have that light inside. There is an awareness of the One who makes things happen, and of who I am and what I have to do. I need to be creating such a pure, elevated awareness all the time.

When you have understanding, and then, using that understanding, you practise bringing it into action, and having practised you have built up experience - then you know what to do, at the right time. That too is a form of light. So, the light increases with experience.

In such a soul it's as if they are constantly seeing inside, so as to learn from everyone and everything that happens around them. They will not have the feeling that they already know everything.

They know they are playing a part, and are very detached in that, but there is also an alertness to keep learning and to avoid mistakes.

When you lose balance and become wrapped up in what you are doing, you can easily miss the signals that tell you the right way forward. Then you fall.

The essence or seed of the knowledge that purifies and renews us is: don't look at the past, or at others; look at God, the true Mother and Father, and then at yourself. Be patient. Remain peaceful. With that true effort, you'll have God's love inside you.

When the Bestower of Knowledge is your companion, at every step He's telling you how things really are. This truth then makes you perform pure, clean, elevated, noble actions. Those actions give power, until you become one who shows truth to the world.

Such a diamond will sparkle from a distance. It won't need to say, "I am a diamond" - its light will automatically and naturally reach far out into the world. When the vibrations of that diamond reach others, they will be comforted and uplifted.

It's truth that has to be revealed. I have to reveal the true Father. But I have to do that with a true heart, with real, honest interest and love.

I say that it's my pure thought that this should happen, but with purity there is no feeling either that I have to do something, or that I have done anything. The truth is in the intention. Then it will be as if I feel a pull internally that tells me what I need to do. And also, what I mustn't do.

The stage of awareness in which I am inside myself, silent and bodiless, sitting with God, makes good things happen outside. It's fixed: there is the awareness that the One who had to get it done is there all the time, and I am just an instrument in between.

The world desperately needs God's love, light and peace – God's truth. God is waiting for us to become so pure that we can be true instruments in sharing these qualities with all souls.

Purity enables me to be detached, and detachment enables me to remain positive, loving and wise.

When I remain in the awareness that I am a spirit, the light and beauty of that spirituality spreads far and wide. When I connect to God's supreme power, it is as if a powerful current flows to where it is most needed.

So, throughout each day, I need to remember:

*1. Do I stay in my spirituality? I am the spirit within, detached from the body. When I maintain this spiritual awareness, the body in which I am sitting will not pull me into performing limited or wrong actions.*

*2. Whilst living in this world, no matter what the atmosphere, situations or events outside, I must remain a detached observer, not passing judgment or taking sides. That way, I'll stay uninfluenced, in my original truth, and the power of that will help others.*

*3. Whilst doing things, I must feel that in reality it was not me that did anything, but that I was an instrument for what needed to happen. That way, I will also remain detached from my actions, so that they don't take hold of me and drain me of energy. Then I'll stay free to keep drawing God's love and wisdom inside me; and others, seeing the power I have gained, will feel inspired to create a similar life for themselves.*

Chapter Four

# The Power of Happiness

PURITY, PEACE, LOVE AND HAPPINESS are deeply connected. Purity is actually the foundation of the other three. The more I attend to it, making sure there is no impurity remaining in me, the more natural my peace will become.

When impurity creeps into the soul, like alloy mixed into gold, I become peaceless. It enters in such a way that I do not notice, and then can't understand why worry, fear and sorrow have become part of my life. It seems as if these negative feelings are simply part of human nature.

It is true that they have formed part of the experience of being human. As such, there is no need for me to feel bad about them. What has happened, has happened.

But when I develop a relationship with God, I receive a mirror that shows me a higher truth. I realise that when I make my thoughts very pure, and then peaceful - nothing ruffled, no disturbance - I can connect with God so deeply that I become the form of love. It's not a question of giving and taking love; I become an embodiment of love.

When I am like this, others feel the love, and it seems to them that this person is very wise and understanding. That is because when I make myself free from wasteful or negative thoughts, I can see clearly what is going on, and what I need to do.

With knowledge about myself and God, I make myself sensible, one with understanding. I make my thoughts pure and peaceful. Then power comes into them. And when someone has power in them, it's as if they suddenly command authority. When I live with the clear consciousness of my eternal identity as a soul, with God's peace and love, I have an authority inside myself.

Purity frees me from body-consciousness. The more successful I am in purity, the more peace and love become a natural part of my form. As I become the form of love myself, it becomes very easy and natural to give love in relationships.

My actions and interactions become based on giving. Since there is a law that what you give, you also receive, the energy of love builds and builds inside me until there is nothing of my old nature remaining. It is as if there is a new nature inside me, based on truth. There is generosity, positivity, and wisdom.

It is actually my original nature. So the feeling is that this relationship with God has allowed me to become who I really am; to be myself. That brings real, lasting happiness.

When we see nature around us - physical nature, with its fields and trees, animals and birds - it automatically gives happiness. It doesn't have to try. In the same way, when my own nature becomes of that quality, through purity and the power of the relationship with God, it gives happiness.

When someone finds happiness somewhere, it really touches the heart. When I experience this type of happiness, the happiness of being, if you like, it makes the happiness received from temporary, worldly attainments seem superficial. Such things won't seem like happiness any longer.

Previously, we used to strive so much to make others happy. And how much effort did others have to make to keep us happy? Time, money, and energy went on such exchanges. We would beat our heads a lot.

When someone upset us, or failed to make us happy in ways we had come to expect, there was hurt and irritation, often causing contempt to grow in the mind. Then, there would be conflict.

Lack of happiness also brought jealousy, and greed. Then we would start to be deceptive, towards ourselves and others. It was as if our natures became impregnated with falsehood. So, what kind of interactions resulted from that?

Now we become free, by realising what we lost, and by filling ourselves again with God's virtues. God likes everybody. He is content and happy with everyone. He sees the wider picture, beyond jealousy and conflict.

When I come close to God, I feel the same. There is the coolness of tolerance inside. This enables me to maintain a clear head, and a warm heart. There is generosity of spirit, and the power to do the right thing.

God Himself is giving me the power to imbibe His virtues. The virtues of God, which the world sings such praises of, are working on me. It's amazing!

It's these virtues that enable me to experience peace, love, and purity, and I feel the joy and happiness of that, a unique joy and happiness. It is a type of happiness that need never run out. I don't have to spend money on it, and nobody can steal it from me.

When I remember certain people for a little while, it pleases the heart and makes me happy. But when I remember God, the feeling is of unlimited happiness. When I act from that happiness, with virtue, the fruit is very sweet and there is joy.

God is taking us on a journey to a high destination, but we are going along laughing and singing with happiness. Of course, obstacles do come, but He just clears the way for us. He's such a wonderful guide, taking great care of us in that way, and that also creates a feeling of happiness inside, when we see how much He helps if we keep Him beside us.

## Detached observer

He tells us: "Soul, remain alone. Just keep looking at Me, the incorporeal One, with the eye of recognition and understanding.

Be detached from everything physical, including your body, and keep me as your companion." Then, you really experience joy.

There's a lot of happiness and joy in understanding your self, and then playing your part as a detached observer. This enables you to play your part well. You never get confused or perplexed, and you remain happy with the other players, interacting with them easily.

Clever actors are the heroes in a drama. They play their part to the full, on the stage, with everybody. But they also keep an eye on the director as he stands in the wings, and are ready to respond to his signals. Others love to watch such actors. The director watches them too, and is proud of them. Such actors experience great lightness in everything they do, because they are happy to be part of such a play.

Purity, peace and love teach me to play my part with happiness. When I experience these qualities, my fellow actors are happy, those watching the play as the audience are happy, and my Director also becomes happy. So, how happy must I be? So happy, as to reveal to the world what happiness really is.

Happiness is such that you can't really explain it. True inner happiness is revealed by the sparkle of your face and features, in the way you walk and move, and how you interact with others.

People with such happiness are radiant, and very real. They have such a feeling of fortune in themselves that their only desire is for everyone else to experience the same. They have the sound inside them, 'let everyone in the world know that One, the Bestower of Fortune, so that each can learn how to create his own fortune.'

This sound reaches others not in the form of preaching, but as a reality, as a gift of truth. Then the fortune multiplies because of the blessings that come back in return.

It is essential to understand the practical benefits of living life in this way. Purity and peace enable me to conquer the vices that used to distort my behaviour and suppress my happiness. Love and happiness, because of the way they benefit others as well as myself, earn me an income as I continue on the pilgrimage towards becoming complete, an angel.

If I am not happy, I will not gain anything. The minute I become unhappy, it's as if there's a hole in my spiritual battery and everything leaks away. Or sometimes there is a blockage: whatever was previously coming to me from God can no longer get in. Then also, everything comes to a standstill, as when the circulation in the body stops because of a blood clot.

This is why God offers us the treasures of happiness. We have the key in our hands. We just have to distribute that treasure. We are equal to the Father, the Lord of the Lords who lives beyond the five elements. He is taking us home, in order that we should rest and that the world should be renewed. So whilst living in this world, in this body, of the five elements, we have to be beyond it. We are only here to give company to others, and lead them back home as well.

"I am going; I am on my way." With such an attitude we will not become trapped by any of our actions or relationships. Our happiness can stay constant and we will be really useful to the world. Even with the vibrations of our thoughts, we can teach people the art of flying along with us. Then, there is success in every task.

When I have no weakness remaining, victory becomes a garland around my neck. With victory inside and success outside, my happiness knows no bounds.

# What is in my heart?

Each one should look at their heart, and examine its condition. What type of feelings do I have in it, for myself and for others? What is the feeling in my heart for the world?

Happiness is connected with the heart, and there is a deep connection between the heart, the brain and vision. Whatever is in the heart will also be in my brain, and will show through my eyes. When my heart is filled with happiness, this will be obvious in my vision. It is as if the eyes share that happiness.

There should be such newness in us, such happiness, as we never even dreamed possible.

For this, the heart must first become absolutely clean. If there's any kind of thorn stuck in it, some pain from the past, that should finish. Don't let there be any type of fear or sorrow from anywhere. What is in my heart? If I have given sorrow to anyone, let me ask for forgiveness in such a way that they are able to forget the sorrow they received from me.

If that forgiveness is not forthcoming, what can I do?

I must check my feelings. Am I really feeling that I want forgiveness from that person? Am I feeling love for them? If I am genuine in this, I should first ask God for forgiveness. Then I can ask that person.

The heart has to be so clean, so honest. Otherwise, my asking for forgiveness will just be another form of taking. There shouldn't be any kind of impatience. My feelings have to be filled with compassion, honesty and love. Realise that these three qualities must be present in my heart. Then the other person will feel these qualities reaching them, as in a donation, and they will accept that you are sincere in regretting what you had done and in wanting to make amends.

Sometimes, I'm not able to experience those qualities of compassion, honesty and love within and towards myself, and so they certainly won't work for others.

The secret then is to check for and remove any trace of selfish feeling. Selfishness blocks my own highest nature, and my connection with God. It gives rise to sorrow, worry or fear within, those negative feelings that destroy my strength and judgment and prevent me from interacting successfully with others.

Then, no matter how hard I may try to project positive feelings, that projection will not work. I cannot give out what I don't have inside.

For true generosity of heart, I need selflessness and honesty. The funny thing is, selflessness is the best possible gift for the self! For if I am selfless in my feelings and motivations, what is there to worry about? I have nothing to lose.

It is certainly no use worrying on behalf of other people. A person who has let go of worry will constantly be engaged in good work, and able to share good feelings; whereas in one who worries, there will definitely be sorrow. Can I have worry and sorrow internally and still be able to share happiness, and enjoy a good night's rest?

In my own life, I have contact with thousands of people. But I always keep the awareness that within my relationships and connections I should have spiritual love, and honesty. This enables the connections to be filled with truth. I have it very clearly in my intellect that this is what I have to do.

When there is that type of connection, filled with pure thoughts and feelings, it will never lead to feelings of fear. There's no need for me to be afraid, nor will anybody be afraid of me.

I've always remembered God out of love and happiness. If you continue to do that, no form of sorrow can come to you, because there's an accumulation of the power of happiness internally.

Understand that this internal happiness really is like an energy. When I practise remembering God, the happiness accumulates and there is the power to keep God as my companion. I am happy, and there is no sorrow.

Whereas sorrow weakens us, happiness brings courage, and faith in the self. These qualities give me strength to carry on doing good work. If there's something good to be done, I'll do it now. And God will enable it to happen. There won't be questions of when or how, stemming from a lack of power. Furthermore, when my actions are genuinely well motivated, there won't be fear or worry.

Remembering God out of sorrow may be a comfort, but it doesn't give strength.

So: finish your sorrow. Remember God with love and happiness, and realise God's nature, how He is. You will find that you are connecting to an ocean of love and happiness. Then you'll realise this is your own nature, too.

It's not a big thing. If you are a mother, you'll know how a mother gives love to a child, and a child gives love to its mother. You know that relationship. There isn't a question of how it happens.

In the same way, imagine how much love God has for His children. His love is wondrous. No one else can have that much love for us. He says, with complete love and truth: "You are Mine."

But I have to accept wholeheartedly that He is mine. When I say, with conviction: "You are my Mother and Father", He becomes the One enabling me to move along in life. He becomes my Teacher, Friend and Guide. This is my own experience.

In India, there is an understanding that a worthy child is one who wants their mother and father to be happy with them. In that lies the child's own happiness. As a result, they constantly experience their parents' blessings. Happiness is sustained and increased all round.

In contrast, if a husband sees that although his wife is living with him, she has love for another man, his heart would have so much sorrow.

In the same way, if I am telling God "I belong to You" but my heart is drawn to a human being, then God also sees this lack of honesty. It's not that He would feel sorrow; but there would be a difference in the love that would reach me, compared with another who was true in their love towards Him. And nobody can give the love that God gives.

God does care, so much. Even at the time of leaving my body, He will look after me on my onward journey. People who have almost gone, and then returned, often testify to this.

## Make God your everything

So, have that much love for God. Open your heart to God, and make God your Mother, Father, Friend, Beloved - your everything. Because when there is this experience you will remain immensely happy. Then the soul will sing a different kind of song. God is the Remover of Sorrow.

And God will say, "This child of mine is so good; he has no concerns or worries or sorrow, and so is constantly happy." It is very good to please God like this.

Friendship with God means you become a friend of the world. When you develop the attitude and feeling that "None but One is mine", you'll receive so much from God that you'll also feel, "Everyone is mine". There will be that connection with everyone, because everyone belongs to God.

Human beings need this power of love and happiness. It can uplift them. Otherwise, they tend to look at each other in ways that give and take sorrow. And if they give happiness, it's only temporary. This sharing from the heart is natural, and lasting.

Somebody who doesn't have sorrow inside will not ask questions like "Why is this person causing me sorrow?" or "Why is this body giving me so much trouble?" He knows that different scenes come to test us, and that consequences of past actions will catch up with us. He is also aware that to feel sorrow is to make matters worse, draining us of the power to do good actions now and in the future.

Sometimes people have such a delicate, sensitive heart that even the slightest pinprick is like a crucifix for them.

Others are so hard-hearted that they don't feel even a drop of mercy for others. They hurl stones, and are so under the influence of anger that they don't realise the damage they are causing. There may not be sorrow immediately, but there will be later.

Who has fear? Those who do wrong things, especially if they say one thing but act totally differently. When you tell lies there is fear.

Or when you steal, or cheat, or defame others.

Understand and realise such things, and by going deep within, bring transformation in the self.

In all instances, the first effort is to remember God with an honest heart. And to remember God with such an honest heart that you never forget to do this work. You may forget other things you have to do, but never this.

When the heart is clean and honest, it stops getting angry or upset, and is then able to realise how others are feeling. The difference is as great as from night into day. People who know you will see the change.

There won't even be the feeling of having to ask for forgiveness for how you used to be, because people will realise you are totally different now.

And if somebody else does something wrong to you, there will be the power to let it go – to forget it, to think nothing has happened, rather than seeking vengeance.

The feeling will grow within of being so honest, so pure and clean-hearted, as to have the strength to shower others with virtue. Then others too will recover the power to tolerate, and develop the ability to change themselves.

This is what true happiness does for us.

Some people have such a nature of experiencing sorrow that even if they are offered something good, something that should bring happiness, they are unable to accept it. People also have the habits of fear and worry.

Sometimes I ask a person with a sad face why they are looking like that. Often, it turns out that some small incident has reminded them of a sorrow experienced years previously, and the memory of that sorrow came flooding back.

They may say, "What do you know of the things I've been through? I've had so much sorrow in the past. People have always treated me like that." If somebody has given them happiness, they won't remember that. So they are actually creating sorrow. Then they don't do anything with courage or faith or trust in themselves.

So, I tell people: first, learn to be happy. People who stay happy and light, free from sorrow and worry, are able to work quickly, with clarity and concentration. When work is done with happiness, with an honest heart, there is this inner strength. They do not have any fear, either, because everybody is happy with them. But when people don't have anything good to think about, the mind becomes occupied with worry and sorrow.

## The worthlessness of worry

Throughout my life, I don't think I have ever had any kind of worry. Even if there was nothing to eat the next day, I would not worry about that. I would have the feeling, whatever happens tomorrow, we'll see tomorrow. At least there's something today. Right now, let me eat with love.

If 50 or 100 people came to my place and I had nothing to feed them, I wouldn't have the thought, "I don't have anything to give them." At least I could welcome them warmly, with a smile, and offer a glass of water. But if my face became worried or sad, I wouldn't even be able to do that.

People are in the habit of pre-empting things, worrying about what might happen. If a child is a bit late coming home from school, the mother may be thinking "Oh, I hope he is OK; I hope he hasn't had an accident." There is fear, and this causes happiness to drain away. Then the mother will not have as much to give. When the child does come home, his happiness may be destroyed if the mother is angry. All this is unnecessary. We have to put an end to habits like these.

Ego also causes happiness to drain away. Ego is so damaging. It is like one of the snakes in snakes and ladders, the board game. You may climb all the way up and then on one of the last squares, ego bites you and makes you come down in one go. If you learn to act with humility, not feeling that you are doing anything but that God enables it to happen, ego will be defeated.

Where there is honesty, there is humility. Where there is falsehood, ego is definitely there. Ego creates falsehood. Honesty and humility give happiness, whereas falsehood and ego take it away. A false person will have ego and with that they'll also have anger. They'll quickly get upset. You have to keep trying to please them. So we don't want to have ego. Don't ask, "How can I finish ego?"

Just have the determined thought, it's something I *have* to do.

In fact, it's renewing your relationship with God, through meditation, that does this for you. It's as if the soul receives a gift from God, to keep the mind peaceful and the heart clean.

When the heart is clean, it means ego is destroyed. When someone has such a clean heart, they are able to learn things very easily. They have self-respect, so they don't run away from their mistakes. They learn from them, and imbibe virtues.

Then the soul develops great stability and clear concentration, because there is honesty within the self.

When the heart is honest, the soul has a lot of strength. A person with pure motives and a selfless attitude receives help from God, directly. They constantly receive guidance and power from God, and they are constantly able to give to others.

A clean and honest heart also becomes naturally generous and cooperative. Consequently, relationships become strong and healthy too.

There won't be any feeling of burden, of having given so much, or any need to speak about how much you've done. There will just be the feeling, "I haven't done anything; it's God who has done everything." And the person who has been helped will feel, "God sent you to me at my time of need."

In this way, happiness becomes unlimited.

Chapter Five

# The Power of
# Divine Truth

WHEN THERE IS the deep realisation of my highest nature, limited desires finish and I am left with just one powerful, overriding feeling: now is the time to become complete.

I have to become so pure inside, so peaceful inside, that I can draw all of God's qualities and virtues into myself. That is my only desire. I become completely, single-mindedly focused on that. And this is what brings power.

Previously, whatever virtues and qualities I had were contaminated with egoism or arrogance. But when I draw strength from God, all the ego inside finishes.

Godly qualities and virtues are extraordinary. They go even beyond human perfection. They are filled with so much energy. They are what is needed in today's world. It's as if we are being called upon to shower the power that comes from those qualities on to the world down here, in this troubled time.

The main qualities that I have to draw from God are truth, and purity. There need to be true feelings in my mind and heart, and pure intentions.

Truth means wholeness – nothing missing, and nothing mixed. Truth is the original quality. God is truth, and the soul is truth. With purity, I am able to experience that truth. When I experience myself as the child of the Mother and Father, I inherit that truth.

Impurity destroys truth. When you experience the power of truth, you understand what a world of difference there is between purity and impurity. The losses caused by impurity become very clear to you.

When the sun's rays are harnessed as solar energy, a special system is needed to receive, store and distribute or use that energy.

In the same way, if I am to receive God's energy and share its power, I need a very pure consciousness.

Firstly, I understand deeply and completely that the energy comes from God. If I forget that, either by turning my back on God or confusing myself with God, I will become directionless and automatically cut myself off from the source. Then I'll be vulnerable again to egoism, addictions, limited desires and the peacelessness that accompanies them.

Secondly, I keep myself in a positive frame of mind, looking for the beauty or the benefit in every scene. This practice enables me to stay doubly light: free from darkness and confusion, and free from burdens. The soul gently flies above obstacles, seeing everything very clearly, as if in a balloon.

Negative thoughts interfere with the flow of this positive energy, and negative feelings, like cold air, cause it to dissipate so that the balloon has difficulty flying.

Negative actions are liable to puncture my spiritual stage altogether, bringing me crashing down. These are actions based on 'low' motives, rooted in bodily desires such as lust and greed. They make me heavy, and I'll find it impossible to fly for as long as their impact lasts. That means it will be hard for me to stay light in myself, let alone bring light and lightness to others.

God's energy is that of true love, and cannot be used to meet selfish or limited ends. If it is used that way, it won't last.

Thirdly, there is the deep desire and will to serve, and to serve unlimitedly. I live with the conviction that we are in an era when all humanity is being uplifted through God's healing power. This is happening, and will definitely continue to happen, but it can't happen without us! It's not a question of a magic wand being waved. According to the time, we are being called upon to do the work of renewing the world with the Mother and Father.

Our own determination is needed, as individuals, to do everything possible to harness and share God's energy. This kind of willpower overcomes our inertia, and all sorts of other obstacles besides.

People have often lost sight of the fact that there is real power within the individual will. When my own thought of doing something is in line with the power of understanding received from God, it can move mountains. There is the feeling that whatever my thoughts, I should put them into practice now.

We need that much willpower, alongside the power of understanding. Willpower comes from within. It means there is no question of "How am I going to do it?" but instead the certainty that God will enable us to do it.

When there is this willpower, and our own inner strength that comes from it, we receive divine power – God's wonderful energy. And this can never fail.

Loss of peace of mind, over a long period, gives rise to sorrow, and that in turn makes us weak. But the reverse is also true.

## Accumulating power

When I resolve to let go of peacelessness, and over a period of time I successfully connect to God, the energy of peace builds inside me and becomes a power.

This power further accumulates as I learn not to be affected by the external events and atmosphere.

When a person is physically strong they develop confidence and courage in their physical capabilities. They develop an attitude of "I can do it."

In the same way, when the experience of fear, sorrow and peacelessness ends, courage and confidence return to my nature. Power develops, enabling me to feel not only that I can rise above obstacles myself, but that I can help others to do the same.

I have received God's love and wisdom. I have used this power practically, and seen the attainments that come from it. All sorts of circumstances appear in front of me but I do not have to suffer. I know that suffering weakens me and prevents me from doing what is needed, whereas maintaining my peace brings success.

My will to be successful has reawoken, and this creates the determined thought and feeling that everything contains benefit. It is not necessary for me to see immediately where the benefit lies. The conviction that good will come from everything that happens enables me to retain my inner power.

Seeing my victory in this, God gives me blessings, which further increase my power. It is as though by holding fast to my peace and positivity, I am able to align myself to God's divine strength and purpose.

By learning to remain peaceful, I automatically free myself from the vices of ego, anger and attachment. This success is much more than an intellectual achievement. It is an empowering experience. It restores in me an inner strength that subtly reaches and helps others, too.

There is no question of the intellect becoming arrogant about this power, because the basis of it is the Divine. When others are served through it, their experience is of support reaching them from God. Similarly, real love is a power that liberates, rather than pulls or binds. Love is not something I can ask for; I myself have to become loving. So I resolve to give love to myself, on the basis of my connection with God, and also in appreciation of the fortune that accumulates in the soul as I learn to live again with truth and love.

I can't lay down the law to others about how to live. That just hurts hearts, and no one will do as I say for long. But God tells me with so much love how to live my own life that the heart feels healed and wants to respond accordingly. It then becomes easy for me to learn, and seeing my example, others will want to do the same.

With pure, divine love, even the biggest of tasks seems small. Such love gets work done. If my love is honest, automatically all tasks turn out well.

The power of truth works through the power of love. If there is the slightest untruth – any form of anger or attachment mixed inside me – love won't work. There won't be success. If there is greed mixed in my love, and I am giving love because I want something, that won't work either.

Love has to be filled with the power of truth, and of non-violence – completely free from any of the pressure caused by selfishness. When I work with this type of love, it brings God's power to me even more. It brings me the power of other people's blessings and goodwill. And the success that comes to me through having used love in the right way also causes my inner power to multiply.

Purity brings power both to the inner world of my thoughts and the outer world of my interactions. When there is purity inside, I will have no desire to deceive anyone. Such honesty and integrity also bring success, both in my personal relationships and in my worldly affairs.

If someone deceives me, I will learn not to let it happen again but I will not allow myself to have feelings of blaming or complaining because that will make me weak.

When purity has been restored inside me, based on the understanding and relationship with the Divine, I will not allow my thoughts to become wasteful in any way, no matter what happens. This is real power!

Equally, I will not allow my thoughts to be pulled in the direction of praise. That will also weaken me by taking me outside of myself.

A pure mind radiates, like the sparkle from a pure, transparent diamond. It is filled with the feeling, "Just as I have received so much, others should receive the same." When others feel this generosity of spirit reaching them, they too will feel uplifted and empowered. Then there is success for everyone.

And I will just want them to take and take, because I'll know that this is God's energy at work, and that it is limitless.

Purity enables me to be real, too, and when something is real there is a lot of power in it.

Purity also makes my nature royal: always giving and generous-hearted, and not asking of others, but commanding a natural influence, loyalty and respect.

Even those with the arrogance of wealth, position or intellect will melt in front of the power of a truly generous heart. Their arrogance breaks, and their eyes open to the realisation that there is so much good they can do to help themselves and others in the future.

# Lasting happiness

Ask people in today's world if they are happy and you will find that they are usually labouring under some difficulties and sorrow, whether in relation to health, finances, relationships or simply within their own mind.

But the happiness that comes from living in the way I have described is constant, because it is not based on anything external.

Money, relationships, even the body – everything can go, and it doesn't matter because we are being carried forward by the power that comes from the consciousness of the Divine. The happiness this brings is itself an energy that moves us forward, through both body and mind.

We are free from worry or fear, too. Since neither people nor possessions out there are giving us happiness, they can't steal happiness from us, either!

If the mind is not happy, it means some aspect of truth has been obscured – one spiritual attainment or another is lacking. There are two main deficiencies of this kind.

One is if I am holding on to any type of desire or want from the external world. If this is not fulfilled, I will become unhappy and therefore weak.

When I understand this very clearly and realise that this weakness prevents me from resolving my unhappiness, I'll find the power to put past hurts behind me and become free from all desires.

The second deficiency that drains me of power is to consider the tasks I am involved with to be a burden, rather than a fortune. Whatever my role at a particular time, there is always benefit within it. When I develop this attitude and awareness I'll become light instead of heavy and power will further accumulate.

No matter what happens, I must not let go of the stability that enables me to keep taking love from God, and giving love to others.

I must realise that if I do let go of it, for whatever reason, I am disempowering myself and my ability to help others as well.

If I resolve that, from this moment onwards, nothing is going to get in the way of my receiving and giving that love, such determination also brings power.

"God is my Father; all are my family; let everybody have happiness." My task is to maintain this consciousness, and not to be affected whether or not other people accept my good wishes.

If someone says something negative and I allow it to enter me and take my own happiness away, that is my weakness.

Once I recognise this, and stop criticising others, I'll know that in order to remove the weakness I either have to draw more power from the Almighty, or pay more attention to using that power in practice. This way, I don't even allow my own shortcomings to cause me sorrow.

And the person or situation that highlights a weakness becomes my teacher and friend, rather than an enemy who can cause me harm. If on the other hand I keep hiding from the mistakes caused by my weakness, they will be repeated.

The wonder of peace, love, purity and happiness is that their vibrations reach everywhere. And that is why the angels have been remembered.

The realisation that enables all these qualities to stay with me constantly in today's world is that they are the soul's inheritance from the Supreme. God, as the Father or Seed of the human family, does have one pure desire: that through knowing Him, all His children should recognise and restore the truth in themselves.

When we live in that truth again, it is as if we become self-sovereigns. The kingdom over which we rule is established by God and nobody can take it from us.

With such strength inside, the only feeling that remains is: let there be happiness for all!

## About the Brahma Kumaris

The Brahma Kumaris is a network of organisations in over 100 countries, with its spiritual headquarters in Mt Abu, India. The University works at all levels of society for positive change. Acknowledging the intrinsic worth and goodness of the inner self, the University teaches a practical method of meditation that helps people to cultivate their inner strengths and values.

The University also offers courses and seminars in such topics as positive thinking, overcoming anger, stress relief and self-esteem, encouraging spirituality in daily life. This spiritual approach is also brought into healthcare, social work, education, prisons and other community settings.

The University's Academy in Mount Abu, Rajasthan, India, offers individuals from all backgrounds a variety of life-long learning opportunities to help them recognise their inherent qualities and abilities in order to make the most of their lives.

**All courses and activities are offered free of charge.**
Visit www.brahmakumaris.org for more information.
www.inspiredstillness.com

# How and Where to Find Out More

## SPIRITUAL HEADQUARTERS
PO Box No 2, Mount Abu 307501, Rajasthan, India
Tel: (+91) 2974-238261 to 68
Fax: (+91) 2974-238883
E-mail: abu@bkivv.org

## INTERNATIONAL CO-ORDINATING OFFICE & REGIONAL OFFICE FOR EUROPE AND THE MIDDLE EAST
Global Co-operation House, 65-69 Pound Lane, London, NW10 2HH, UK
Tel: (+44) 20-8727-3350
Fax: (+44) 20-8727-3351
E-mail: london@brahmakumaris.org

# REGIONAL OFFICES

## AFRICA

Global Museum for a Better World, Maua Close,
off Parklands Road, Westlands, PO Box 123, Sarit Centre, Nairobi, Kenya
Tel: (+254) 20-374-3572
Fax: (+254) 20-374-3885
E-mail: nairobi@brahmakumaris.org

## AUSTRALIA AND SOUTH EAST ASIA

181 First Ave, Five Dock, Sydney, 2046 Australia
Tel: (+61) 2 9716-7066
E-mail: ashfield@au.brahmakumaris.org

## THE AMERICAS AND THE CARIBBEAN

Global Harmony House, 46 S. Middle Neck Road,
Great Neck, NY 11021, USA
Tel: (+1) 516-773-0971
Fax: (+1) 516-773-0976
E-mail: newyork@brahmakumaris.org

## RUSSIA, CIS AND THE BALTIC COUNTRIES

2, Lobachika, Bldg. No. 2, Moscow – 107140, Russia
Tel: (+7): +7499 2646276
Fax: (+7) 495-261-3224
E-mail: moscow@brahmakumaris.org